CW01433021

Be the Noodle

50 Ways to be a Compassionate, Courageous, Crazy-Good Caregiver

Lois Kelly

Copyright ©2020 Lois Kelly

All rights reserved.

DEDICATION

In memory of Elizabeth (Bette) Kelly
Everything is possible in a whatever world.

In honor of my remarkable family
Together we're extraordinary. Except for the singing thing.
This story belongs to all of us.

CONTENTS

1 CAREGIVERS NEED AN ADVENTURE GUIDE

I first published this book 10 years ago because I wanted people helping a loved one die to know that they're not alone. I wanted to share my experience helping my mother die so that people might find the courage, love and sick humor to be fully present with the person they love. To make a sad part of life, a treasured part of life.

I am so humbled and joyful knowing that this little book has done just that for many. I am also grateful that people have been kind enough to tell me how the book affected their lives. And that they wanted it to be reissued.

One of my favorite stories about the book's impact came from a family in Alabama.

> Kelli was at college, away from her parents, sick with worry and grief about her dying father. She read *Be the Noodle* and sent it to her mother.
>
> Her mother read this book and called her daughter: "Come right home."
>
> A few months later Kelli's mother wrote to me. "I had no intention of sharing with Kelli or her brother the last 15 days when the dying had begun. My husband and I did not want

those memories to be our children's last memoires of their father.

"But when Kelly insisted I read *Be the Noodle*, I realized I had to allow her to part of the most agonizing, poignant, intimate, and life-changing experience of our lives.

"Thank you for helping us remember my husband's final days not with agony and heart break but as his caregiver, the 'most courageous, inspiring and rewarding job I never wanted.'"

Be the Noodle is a caregiver's adventure guide, based on my wild, wondrous and life changing journey helping my mother die at home.

A lot of people have said, "Why write about something so depressing?" The answer is that helping someone during their final months can be inspiring and rewarding in ways that you never thought possible. You can find superpowers that you never knew you had. While this is about dying, it's also about possibilities.

An adventure is defined as an experience that can be both terrifying and inspiring because you enter into a flow that is like nothing you've ever experienced before. Helping someone die can be one of life's greatest adventures.

I hope that some of the 50 lessons in this book help you navigate the adventure and become a compassionate, crazy-good caregiver, one of the most courageous jobs you never wanted.

With joy and gratitude,

Lois Kelly

PS – Remember to pay it forward, passing the book along to someone who has entered the caregiver journey. They will appreciate it much more than a banana bread or casserole.

2 SWIMMING TOO FAR OUT

My mother and I are sitting on a stretcher in the basement hallway of Mass General Hospital. Our winter coats are piled in a heap next to us. It's 12:30 in the morning, dark and frigid outside, but in the bowels of this giant Boston hospital it is bright, hot and chaotic.

The fluorescent overhead lights are loud, making a buzzing sound like those annoying bug zappers you hear in the summer. The woman on the gurney across the hall is telling the emergency room physician that she has no friends or family in the United States. Just her boyfriend, who earlier in the day broke her neck and nose. Next to us an elderly woman with gnarly hands and green eyes moans alone.

A camera crew from ABC-TV is dodging the incoming patients, looking for people to interview for a documentary on urban hospitals.

"How about us," asks my mother Bette, as in Bette Davis. "We've got a good story now." They ignore us, two middle-class, nicely dressed women laughing and talking amid so much human drama.

Ninety minutes ago, the doctors told Bette that the headaches and vision problems she's been having are cancer. In fact, her head is loaded with malignant tumors. Not one, not two, but many.

Next stop: the neuro-oncology ward for more questions, more tests, and more experts. The only certain thing is that Bette's long-term prognosis is not good.

As we sit waiting for a hospital room to open up Bette turns to me and says, "We can do this. It won't be easy, but we can. I know we can."

Bette has decided that she doesn't want to spend the rest of her life in hospitals or be sick any more than is likely to eventually happen.

"I'll be open to what the specialists have to say tomorrow," she says. "But what I really want is to go home and live at my little house and walk the beach as much as I can. I don't want to live the rest of my life sick from treatments to prolong my life for who knows how long. I know you all will help me do this."

In this case "do," meant that Bette would do everything in her power to help us help her. But no hospitals. No live-in medical help. No extraordinary measures. Just living at home as comfortably as possible, cared for by family instead of medical clinicians. (This was not the time to tell her I couldn't even help my son when he got sick to his stomach; how the heck was I going to be able to do this cancer thing?)

I believed Bette that early morning in the hospital basement as I have always believed my mother when she was convinced something was possible. It was a pattern of our lives.

Bette's belief that "we can do this" was like her unwavering belief that if you know how to swim, you'll be fine even when you swim too far out and the current starts pulling.

My late father would sit on the beach worrying as Bette swam out into the ocean. What if she got a cramp? Got caught in a strong current? Who could save her then?

"Why can't she stay closer in or use one of those swimming noodles like other people who go far out," he'd ask us as we watched Bette swim further and further out to the horizon.

My father was referring to the Styrofoam swimming noodles that you see littered all over the beach in hard-to-miss fluorescent green, yellow and purple colors. Those Styrofoam swimming noodles don't look sturdy or safe, but they give you a weird kind of support even though you still have to use your arms and legs.

Bette paid her husband no attention, believing in her soul that there was nothing to worry about when you're swimming. Worse case you turn over and float on your back, letting the buoyancy and goodness of the salt-water guide you back to shore. You don't need silly little children's noodles to help you swim, especially in the ocean.

But Bette, so independent and headstrong throughout her life, already knew that this final stage would not be an easy swim. Cancer currents are filled with rip tides, sandbars, the occasional shark, and way too many jellyfish lurking in the seaweed. She would have to hold on to a noodle. And that noodle would be her family and friends, helping her stay buoyant despite   unpredictable currents, pulling her to safety when she could no longer paddle.

My father really believed that Bette would die from swimming too far out by herself. Not from cancer. He would have been surprised to learn that Bette finally agreed to hold on to a noodle.

Caregiver Lesson #1

Be the noodle.

3 ADVOCATING FOR MARTINIS

We were in a rush and feeling overwhelmed and disorganized that Thursday morning at Mass General Hospital.

It had been six days since Bette had had major neurosurgery to remove the largest of her brain tumors, and less than 24 hours since she learned that the real source of her cancer was in her lungs, from which the cancer had spread to her brain. We had thought the cancer had been just those six or 10 malignant brain tumors and that surgery had removed the biggest of those tumors, buying time.

What now?

Well, the most immediate "what now" was the nurse announcing that my mother was being discharged? She could go home.

"Today? With all these staples in my head?" Bette asked. (There were 56 of those suckers in the back of her head, crusted with dried blood, holding her skull together, still at great risk of infection.)

"Yes, now. Do you have someone who can drive you to the Cape?"

Bette had no clothes, but I had a car. We were making a break. Getting her out of Sickville to her home near the beach might just be the best possible medicine at this point.

We figured out how to wrap her up in blankets over those flimsy little hospital johnnies and decided that not having shoes wasn't going to be an issue. The hospital socks would keep her feet warm.

I'd pull the car up to the hospital door and we'd get help getting her in the car, avoiding the early March slush.

I called my uncle to ask him to turn on the heat at Mum's house. The nurse came in with pages of post-op instructions; lists of medications, a schedule for follows up visits.

It was overwhelming.

Then my sister Nancy, a nurse practitioner, arrived, followed by the neurosurgeon, who wanted to review all the instructions with Bette.

Nancy was able to help my mother understand the implications of what the doctor was explaining and reassured us that she'd be down the Cape the next day to help sort out all the medications.

"Is there anything else," the neurosurgeon asked.

"Is it alright for Bette to have a martini," asked Nancy.

"A martini?"

"Yes," said Nancy. "My mother has always enjoyed a martini at night before dinner. Can she drink a martini?"

"Well, err, ah, I don't know. I guess it can't do any harm," replied the doctor.

With that my mother thanked the surgeon for all he had done for her, got in the wheelchair, and away we went. Two fugitives speeding down Boston's southeast expressway before rush hour, feeling like Thelma and Louise.

When we got to my mother's small town early that evening, we stopped at the pharmacy to get the drugs, the grocery store to get gourmet take out, and then scooted to the liquor store to get some vermouth and vodka.

At home that night Bette was elated. She was home, able to sleep in her own bed, her own quiet bedroom. No doctors, no tests, no other sick people.

She lifted up her martini glass and toasted, "To Home."

I lifted my beer and toasted. "To Nancy, who knows all the right medical questions to ask."

Now that's a patient advocate.

Caregiver Lesson #2

Don't be afraid to ask the stupid questions that can make a person happy. Like martinis.

4 PRIVATE BENJAMIN REPORTING FOR CAREGIVING DUTY

I've always hated the war metaphor used in sports and business.

What's the company's mission and target? Seize the opportunity. Defend your position. Every battle is won before it is fought. Capture market share. Establish a beachhead and expand. Focus on the blocking and tackling. Hit the ground running.

Especially that last one. It makes me think of a fire alarm ringing in an office and all of sudden everyone jumps out of their cubicles, falls to the floor, and starts running, crouched down low like they're avoiding an ambush.

No one is going to die if you lose a football game or close a business deal.

But becoming a caregiver for someone with a terminal illness deserves the war metaphor. This really is life or death. The stakes are high. The enemy – that sneaky, unpredictable disease – is wily, hiding in the overgrowth, launching surprise attacks all the time.

And we caregivers, well we're like Private Judy Benjamin, the Goldie Hawn character in the 1980 movie Private Benjamin. Judy Benjamin is a spoiled dingbat who admits she "is 29 years-old and trained to do nothing."

We become caregivers thinking that we can do this. How hard could it be?

And like Private Benjamin, we know we're in trouble on the very first day when we're thrown into combat without any basic training, operating new equipment, taking orders from higher-ups, following new rules, and battling sleepless nights and days of looking like hell because there's just no time to take care of ourselves.

And, of course, there's the latrine duty, KP, guard duty and all the other nasty, repetitious assignments that you just have to be able to double down and do 100 percent.

There's really no escape. You're on duty.

There's no tough drill sergeant to tell you what to do when it comes to helping someone with a serious illness. You volunteered for an assignment that has no rules, regulations or training. You, like Judy Benjamin, wonder, "What the heck have I committed to? I have no idea what I'm doing."

That's how I feel, having volunteered to live during the week with my mother for the duration. I could do this because my marketing consulting work gave me more flexibility than family members with 9-to-5 type jobs.

But could I really do this?

The army recruiter tells Private Benjamin that she can be "all that she can be."

Ditto for being drafted as a caregiver.

Caregiver Lesson #3

No special skills necessary. You'll learn on the job.

5 ENOUGH OF THE BANANA BREAD

Birthdays: cake

New Year's Eve: champagne

Terminal cancer diagnosis: banana bread?!

OK, I know this sounds ungrateful. But hold off on the banana bread. Sick people rarely have a sweet tooth and the caregiver rarely can eat all those banana breads.

The week Bette got home from Mass General Hospital, people kept stopping by the house and leaving banana bread. We must have had nine loaves by the end of the week, and three big plates of brownies. It seemed like the banana breads were reproducing. Every morning there would be more. I came down to the kitchen, made coffee, and pondered, "What should I do with the banana bread?"

I started freezing it. But then there was no room in the freezer for real food.

Clearly stressed about the multiplying banana breads and feeling guilty about throwing kind intentions into the trash, I asked one of my mother's friends, "Why are people giving us so much banana bread?"

"It's so that you have something on hand to give people when people visit," she explained.

"But Bette is too sick for visitors. I'm the only one here."

"Oh."

After people die, there are a lot of people around who need to be fed. While people are dying at home and not wanting any visitors, there's not much need for banana bread.

 A better option would be to ask the caregiver what food, from what local stores or takeout restaurants she might like. Really, it's OK to ask. During these days with my mother, the last thing I want to do is to grocery shop and cook. But I need to make sure she eats, and I'm always hungry.

To be able to have the squash and steak tips from a favorite restaurant is heaven. Better yet, put us on a steady diet of deliveries from the local caterer. Even better, instead of saying, "Let me know how I can help," offer to organize friends to drop off home cooked meals on a schedule.

The ill person needs to eat to keep some strength and be able to tolerate medications; the caregiver needs to eat to stay healthy to be able to care.

Just not banana bread.

Caregiver Lesson #4

Tell all those generous friends and neighbors what kind of food you would appreciate. Otherwise, beware the banana bread bombardment.

6 BOO BOO'S MOTHER-IN-LAW'S NEXT-DOOR NEIGHBOR'S COUSIN HAD CANCER TOO

When it came time to spread the news of my mother's illness to my co-workers and friends, I wasn't sure what to say or how to say it and didn't want the spotlight on me.

I shouldn't have been concerned. Everyone knows someone who knows someone who had cancer or some other terminal illness.

You share your news and people say, "You know, Boo Boo's mother-in-law's next door neighbor's cousin had lung cancer and went to a hospital and was wicked sick so she got chemotherapy that made her bald, then died, and her daughter was wicked exhausted so be careful and make sure you take care of yourself."

This was not easy to hear.

I didn't care about Boo Boo. Still don't. Never will.

One person listened to me – and listened hard. Then kind words of advice followed. I think of them when I sit quietly with my mother.

"Ask your mother questions. Find out as much as you can about her. Ask what her life has been like."

Everyone's story and experience are different. Listen. Don't talk.

That's what people on the front lines need the most.

From Nancy Kelly

Caregiver Lesson #5

Avoid the chatty Cathy know-it-alls. Seek out those who will simply listen with you for a while.

7 TEA BUT NO SYMPATHY

Getting the news that someone you love has an incurable disease is like being shot into a bizarre parallel universe. First you keep trying to make sense of it all. How could it be the world I knew no longer exists? What will life be without the person I love so much?

Just as you're trying to make sense of this new life that you never intended and never wanted, you get slammed by well- intentioned people smothering you and your loved one with platitudes.

(The definition of platitude is "a pointless, unoriginal or empty comment or statement made as though it were significant or helpful.")

"I can deal with the cancer," said Bette, "but PLEASE spare me the sympathy. I can't stand it when people give me these pitying looks and tell me things like 'I know how you must feel. But you have to be strong and hopeful. Sometimes people live much longer than the doctors ever expect.' I'm OK with dying, why can't they be?"

I witnessed one such sympathy encounter. While my mother's manners prevent her from ever being rude, I could read her body language and tone of voice, which, if translated, would have gone something like: "Get this boob the hell out of here. She has no idea what it's like to be told you're dying. Telling me to 'have hope' is so condescendingly stupid and inane. And she just seems to keep blabbing on and on about nothing, which is exhausting. This is why I'm starting to dread visitors."

So, a few things to avoid:

- I'm so, so sorry. I can't believe this is happening to someone like you.

- Oh my God, what are you going to do?

- Have you talked with your doctor about homeopathic, alternative medicine treatments? You know there are a lot of options out there that doctors don't know about.

- This is a time where you must have faith in God.

- You must feel so grateful that your children are nearby.

What is helpful:

- Simply say, "I heard the news." Then let the ill person or the caregiver respond. She or he will likely direct the conversation towards what is comfortable for them. And remember, this is about them and not about you.

- Pick up on the cues.

- Often, I hear my mother say to someone, "Let's not talk about that." That's the request to please, please NOT talk about that topic. Drop it. Avoid it like the plague or the metastatic cancer that it is.

When visiting bring a plant, bring a book, bring some good English tea.

But please, no sympathy.

Caregiver Lesson #6

Be a sherpa guide for visitors, suggesting what to talk about and what to avoid.

8 FRUSTRATION: 10 THINGS DOCTORS WON'T TELL YOU

My mother taught us all how to be planners.

There is nothing a person can't accomplish, she taught us young, if you just make a plan, figure out the 'to do' list, set deadlines, tick 'the done' tasks off the list, and before you know it – mission completed.

Except for this dying thing.

You can't make a plan, can't get the answers you want, and have no idea what to expect. For we Type A's this is torture. I go to the oncologist's office with my list of questions, eager to make a plan only to hear the following.

1. How long is does the ill person have to live? (Everyone is different; it's difficult to say.)

2. What patterns should we expect as the illness progresses? (Everyone is different; it's difficult to say.)

3. When did the disease start? (Everyone is different; it's difficult to say.)

4. What is panic worthy? What should really worry me as a caregiver and what is "normal" under these abnormal circumstances? (Everyone is different; it's difficult to say.)

5. Does she really need to take 28 different medicines at four different times a day? (Everyone is different; it's difficult to say.)

6. Would radiation or chemo help her make it through the summer? One last summer at the beach would make us all so happy. (Everyone is different; it's difficult to say.)

7. Will we need to hire special aides or nurses to help us when the messy body malfunctions kick in? (Everyone is different; it's difficult to say.)

8. How much will she suffer at the very end, when she can't express pain? (Everyone is different; it's difficult to say.)

9. When should we give up on chemo and radiation? When do we know that any treatment isn't going to extend Mum's life or give her a better quality of lie? (Everyone is different; it's difficult to say.)

10. When should we stop giving her the pills that are for things other than the cancer, like high blood pressure? (Everyone is different; it's difficult to say.)

Caregiver Lesson #7

There are no answers or certainties. Know you'll know what to do when you need to do it.

9 YOUR VALET IS HERE TO SERVE YOU

Today Bette and I feel like we're on vacation. Who knew that this dying thing can be filled with so many "feeling good" days?

I walk on the beach early in the morning despite the cold March wind and come back to the house to find Mum cooking me my favorite omelet – spinach, olives, feta cheese and tomato. After eating and doing the crossword puzzle together I go upstairs to the den to work and Mum turns on "The Today Show" or reads a book.

Bette agreed to neurosurgery because the oncologists thought that she would be able to read again if they could remove the biggest of the brain tumors.   Everyone defines "quality of life" while living with cancer differently. Bette said no to chemotherapy, but yes to an even more invasive treatment because it meant being able to read, which is so central to her life.

"What would I ever be able to do these days if I couldn't read," she wonders with gratitude.

Bette reads and naps during the day as I work. Later in the day I make Mum a martini and bring our dinner into the living room on trays with the fancy linen napkins that we use to save for special occasions.

"Oh nurse," laughs Mum. "Could you get me some more water?"

"I am your *valet*, here to serve you," I reply

"Oh, I like that title much better," says Bette. "Makes me feel like I'm not a burden and that I don't really have cancer."

Being a valet makes it easier for this rookie caregiver, too. I know nothing about caregiving and the very word intimidates and depresses me. Valet? That sounds like something I can do.

I read somewhere that labeling influences a person's behavior. Labeling myself as a valet keeps us both feeling positive. And when the good days turn into bad days, calling for the valet makes us laugh.

"Could the valet serve me in bed today?" "At your service, Ma'am."

Caregiver Lesson #9

Be a valet, not a nurse.

10 I WANT TO HOLD YOUR HAND

Easter was a tough day for Bette. She knew it would be the last holiday with her family, all those big and little grandchildren, nieces and nephews, children, sister, brothers, in-laws and out-laws. (As we lovingly refer to some of the in-laws.)

But she rallied, despite her exhaustion, despite feeling melancholy, despite the swelling in her legs.

She wore a beautiful new robin's egg blue vest, the same color as her eyes, got the eyeliner on remarkably even, and wore a perfect rose-colored lipstick. Though thin she looked like a healthy person.

The afternoon visiting at her brother's house was tough. She was so tired. She felt like people were fawning over her and paying their last respects.

I sat down on the couch next to her and asked, "You doing OK?"

"I feel like I should be wearing a sign that says, 'Last Chance,'" she said.

I took her hand and held it.

"Thank you, that's what I need," she said.

When we protect and reassure our babies, we hold their hands. When we are in love, we hold our lovers' hands, silently signaling our commitment, our devotion, our caring. But somehow, we fall out of the habit of holding hands. We forget the magic of such a simple gesture.

Caregiver Lesson #9

Hold hands.

11 SHE'S GOT THE POWER

Bette, like most healthy or sick people, wants to call all her own shots. It's her life and she's making decisions on the big things like whether to have surgery or do chemo, to the small things, like whether it's a good day for visitors or if the screens should be put on the windows now or after pollen season.

Sometimes as caregiver it's hard not to control and coddle. Caring for someone so sick often feels like caring for a newborn. Their vulnerability and physical dependencies trick us into thinking that they're incapable.

Some days I question Bette's decisions.

"I am in charge of me until I can't be," she says. End of conversation. "I'm an adult, not some child just because I have cancer."

If there was a soundtrack for the sick person's desire to be in control, it would be the 1990's dance song, "The Power" by Snap!, which has become a cult-like anthem at sporting events.

I imagine that Bette has the energy to get up and dance. She's ready to tear down the house and party to her theme song. Cue the music and turn the volume way up when the staccato synthesizers kick in.

Here's Bette singing (to paraphrase the lyrics as best I can):

I've got the power hey yeah heh

I've got the power

Oh-oh-oh-oh-oh-oh-oh-oh-oh yeah-eah-eah-eah-eah-eah

I've got the power

Oh-oh-oh-oh-oh-oh-oh-oh-oh yeah-eah-eah-eah-eah-eah

Gettin' kinda heavy

It's gettin' it's gettin' it's gettin' kinda hectic It's gettin' it's gettin' it's gettin' kinda hectic It's gettin' it's gettin' it's gettin' kinda hectic It's gettin' it's gettin' it's gettin' kinda hectic

Now keep that song in your head as situations arise where you feel strongly about what should be done and the person you love disagrees with you. Who's got the power? Not you. You're just here to help. Here comes Bette singing in our faces again.

> *I've got the power*
>
> *Oh-oh-oh-oh-oh-oh-oh-oh-oh yeah-eah-eah-eah-eah-eah*

If doctors or hospice nurses look at you instead of talking directly to the person who's sick, change the lyrics and sing baby, sing.

> *She's got the power*
>
> *Oh-oh-oh-oh-oh-oh-oh-oh-oh yeah-eah-eah-eah-eah-eah*

Caregiver Lesson #10

You're not in charge. Let the dying person lead.

12 THE JOY OF NOTES AND CARDS

People call every day and ask me, "What can I do?"

I tell them that now is the time to tell the dying person how much he or she has meant to you, how much you have learned from her. This is such a gift. A BIG, BIG gift.

It lifts the spirits around the house.   When I open the mailbox after lunch and find these notes for Bette, p23 I know it will be a good day.

It needn't be long. Just a short note. People who are very ill love receiving cards and notes.

My mother keeps a large basket of notes in the living room, taking such comfort from all her friends.

"Have you seen all these cards," Bette asks me. "It's just unbelievable. I never knew there were so many people who cared so much about me. Aside from my family, I'm most proud about these cards, these people who have written to me. I just never knew that there were this many people in my life."

What's been so nice – and it's another big lesson for me – is to keep sending cards. Many days the ill person wants no visitors, is too weak to talk on the phone, but so appreciates opening a new card and receiving a warm "Hi" from a friend.

Cards are also a way for people to say things that can be hard to say in person. Like just how much you love them or what they have meant to your life.

Betté keeps a card from her niece Amy on the bedroom bureau, sharing it selectively with close family members. It fills her with joy.

Dear Aunt Bette,

I am so sad. I can't imagine what life is going to be without you. My sisters and I have learned so much from you on how to be the best aunt.

You and Uncle Jim have always been such important people in my life, and I will always make sure that I care for and love my nieces and nephews the way you and Uncle Jim have done for us. When I remember what you've done for me and do the same with my nieces and nephews I will smile.

Love you, Amy

Caregiver Lesson #11

Tell people how much their cards and notes mean – and ask them to keep them coming.

13 DENIAL IS A VAMPIRE

Playing "let's pretend" is a game for children. "Now, you pretend that you're an astronaut lost in space, and I'm mission control...."

But adults playing "pretend" drags down the terminally ill person and the caregivers. Acting like everything is normal may help you cope with your sadness, but those good intentions are cloaked in denial, and that denial is a really bad-ass energy vampire sucking the life from the dying person and the caregivers. Once again, we have to explain the real deal to you.

Hear the energy suck, making us so weary.

One of Bette's friends explained that their investment club was moving the June meeting to a location halfway between Boston and the Cape to make it easier for Bette to attend.

Bette was astounded. Truly. She had told her friend how ill she was, dying really. Could she have been franker? What's with the denial?

"I really don't think I'll be in any shape to go," said Bette.

"Well maybe instead of dinner we could change it to lunch if that would be easier," said her friend.

"Really, don't plan around me. I'm in no condition to be planning eight weeks out," said Bette, exhausted from having to again remind people how very sick she is.

When in doubt with a terminally ill person, look at him or her. I mean really take a close look. Is their speech slower than usual? What about their body language – perhaps more stooped in the shoulders? Are they walking more cautiously and slowly? Are their clothes hanging off a bit? Do they eat much? What about the eyelids? Probably a bit drooped.

When you hear someone is very ill, be more aware, and then respect what you see. Even more, respect what the person says.

Instead of presuming, ask gently, "Do you think you might be up for going to an investment meeting in the coming weeks?"

Then listen. The terminally ill person will tell you whether she thinks it's possible, or to please count her out.

Flash forward from kids' playing pretend to teenagers denying what they were really up to while you were out on Saturday night. Ah, you can sniff the denial. And it's making you angry, bad-ass angry.

Denial often rips our guts out. Never mind our hearts.

That's how we feel when people refuse to accept the real deal.

Caregiver Lesson #12

Take people aside and explain the reality of the illness, and that you're trying to keep the house free of denial vampires.

14 WHICH HOUSE WILL THEY BUY? JELL-O BRAIN KNOWS

Something happens to your brain during the caregiving journey. The brain goes from being a reliable Energizer battery to green Jell-O® with pieces of canned pears jiggling all around.

Jell-O brain makes it hard to work, to plan, to read. At night after Bette falls asleep, I go to my addiction – House & Garden TV. (HGTV for short.)

Mind you, I try not to watch it every night, late into the night, and I don't watch the HGTV program about improving a house's curb appeal. Who cares about the outside of the house?

But the shows where people look at three different houses and choose one to buy is a favorite. (Hint: if you're stressed for time you can tune in at ten minutes to the hour and get a summary of all three houses and see the winner.)

This house hunting show provides entertainment when all the sisters are together. It's the one program we all like. No debate, simply mindless communal fun.

"Look at that house. It's so ugly," someone shouts at the TV. "Look at the brown cabinets in the kitchen. Brown with the rose-colored counters and a blue tiled floor? That's a deal killer."

"Why would two people need a 6,300 square foot home? I mean, two people with six bathrooms? That's ridiculous." "Imagine having to clean six bathrooms every week?"

"I bet they're going to buy house #3. Who wants to bet?"

HGTV is mindless entertainment. Easier than having to concentrate on a movie or a book. Or trying to have a conversation. The voyeuristic element where you get to see how people live and decorate is such a good distraction.

But when my sisters are gone and I watch HGTV alone, my mind wanders.

"Which house will the Johnsons buy?" asks the perky HGTV lady.

Which week will Mum die?

"Will it be the 2,600 square foot contemporary 60's ranch?"

Will it be before Andrew's graduation?

"Will it be the much smaller 1,800 square foot classic craftsman with the pool?"

Will she make it through summer, one last summer at the beach?

"Or will the Johnsons choose the larger townhouse close to downtown with city views?"

Or will she decide to go before Memorial Day so none of us have to change our summer plans?

During the day while we're on active duty we're too busy to think. At night with just the glow of the TV lighting the living room the questions pop.

There are no answers. But I'm always pretty good at guessing which house the Johnsons and all the other HGTV house hunters will choose. Even with Jell-O brain.

That is my only super-power for predicting these days. All other bets are off.

Caregiver Lesson #13

Super caregivers need not have superpowers. Kind Jell-O brains are as qualified as brainy brains.

15 PHOTO DISTRACTIONS

Last week Joann came down and brought a photo of all the neighborhood kids eating watermelon in our backyard in the summer of 1964.

The photo got Bette and Joann to talking about all those "kids" and remembering what it was like on Newport St., where the families were big, the houses were small, and the money was tight.   But somehow life was OK. In fact, Bette says those were some of the happiest days in her life.

All the neighborhood mothers seemed united. The rules for the neighborhood kids were the rules, like the parents had gotten together and made a pact, written a special code of conduct for that one block of that one street. Values, punishment and rewards seemed consistent from family to family. Talk about a tribe.

Yet those same parents sure acted like kids, turning cold, unfinished basements into party spaces. Staying up late drinking beer and playing bridge on Friday nights.

And let's not forget that one father who put firecrackers in an outhouse during a summer vacation when we all migrated from Boston to New Hampshire. Sometimes the kids felt like the parents, yet we didn't know what the rules were supposed to be. So, we just ran wild too.

On weeknights the mothers were often out the door as soon as the fathers pulled up the driveways and the kids were fed. I remember my mother taking evening sewing classes and making us such beautiful outfits. The hounds-tooth skirt, coat and matching hat for Easter were my favorites. We couldn't afford Filene's, but Bette made us originals.

See the 1964 watermelon photo has been good for Bette and all of us.

A good photograph is a wonderful distraction. It takes you somewhere else, far from the 'Mum-is-dying-soon" reality. Photographs trigger all kinds of memories, mostly good, some not so good, but now is the time to talk about those too. Tick tock.

Forget about baking brownies – or banana bread. Dig through those old photo albums and bring one really great picture.

Caregiver Lesson #14

Escape into old photographs.

16 THELMA AND LOUISE HIT THE ROAD, AGAIN

(This time my sister Nancy is driving....)

I really shouldn't drive. I've been half blind for 18 years, but the sun was out, and the car had gas. My mother really shouldn't drive either; she is now half blind on the other side. Two bad brains equal one good brain. We pulled out of the driveway and headed for the beach.

The sun was high, the wind was low. We drove slowly. The beach was empty. Bette is so stubborn that she practiced her balance walking on the sand. We got to the water's edge, she held my arm, stooped down, put her hand in the water, and sighed. We surveyed the beach, looked out at the Vineyard in the horizon, and we decided it was a good day.

Whenever it is my mother and me, without the others who would recommend that they drive, we get in the car posing as Thelma and Louise. We're not sure who is who. We know the beach is there and it is waiting for us to declare the day as good.

Caregiver Lesson #15

Enjoy small indulgences and declare the day good.

17 THE CAREGIVER SOUNDTRACK

Some days while caring for my mother I feel lost. Maybe disoriented is a better word. There's no predicting how she will be from one day to the next. I fear I'm letting my business colleagues down by spending too much time away from work. And then there's my husband and 14-year-old son at home, probably eating pasta and no vegetables again for the fourth or seventh time this week.

Walks help. But music helps me more. Some days the music allows me to wallow in my "lost-ness" while driving alone to the grocery store.

Other days my caregiver soundtrack makes me feel strong and courageous and oh-so-positive. Bring it on, I can handle it.

Social workers advise caregivers to make sure they take care of themselves. Here's the soundtrack that's caring for me:

Mercy Angel by Brian Blade

And So It Goes by Bill Joel

Don't Give Up by Kate Bush and Peter Gabriel

Trouble by Cat Stevens

Tenderly by Duke Ellington

Stay by Jackson Browne

Beauty Mark by Rufus Wainwright

The Way by Neil Young

Holy Holy by Marvin Gaye

I Will Survive by Gloria Gaynor

The Surest Things Can Change by Gino Vannelli

Reach Out and I'll Be There by The Four Tops

Friends by Elton John

A Song for You by Donny Hathaway

We Can't Be Someone Else by Arling & Cameron

Angel by Aretha Franklin

You Get What You Give by New Radicals

What'll I Do by The McGarrigle Family

Caregiver Lesson #16

Surrender to the music you love.

18 JUST BEING THERE

Here's a valuable gift to give to the person you love: just be around.

A presence in the house reassures. Simply folding clothes while you watch the morning talk shows can be more than enough. Or being upstairs working in the den while Mum sleeps most of the day.

"I wish you would go home and be with your family," Bette says every week, several times a week.

As always, I say nothing because Bette's follow-up line comes on cue after a short pause.

"But I'm so happy you're here. I know I'm being selfish, but it makes me so happy having you."

Them on cue I say, "No, Mum, I'm being selfish. I want to be with you. I want to be with you longer than I'm going to get being with you."

Our talk sometimes leads to the things we're no longer going to be able to do together. Scrabble games out on the deck, theater in Providence, late summer afternoons on the beach.

"How lucky I have been to do all these things with all of you," Bette often says, meaning sons, daughters, sister, brothers, aunts, uncles and friends.

"Now, go do your work or some errands while I nap."

Caregiver Lesson #17

Being there is doing.

19 THERE WILL BE ANGRY WORDS

My youngest sister, a successful, buttoned-up business professional, can juggle a zillion things at once. One Friday she called to report on Mum's meeting with the oncologist in Boston.

"We had a good meeting with the oncologist today. He thinks radiology can shrink the brain tumors and then chemo can help with the lung cancer. And we might be able to do the chemo down the Cape, so Mum doesn't have to come up to Boston. The next appointment is ...."

"Stop," I snapped. "Maybe all this treatment isn't right. Maybe it's going to make Mum sicker and ruin her quality of life, the one thing she wants. You're pushing her too fast."

Radio silence.

My sister was angry. Pissed is probably more accurate. She had taken the day off from work and shepherded Bette through all kinds of appointments, taking notes, being there. What right did I, who wasn't there, have to contradict her?

We icily closed the conversation, saying we'd talk later.

I felt awful, but my sister's take-charge approach felt controlling to me that day, too black-and-white, too decisive. Like she was in control and not Bette. And, of course, I'm sure I came across as the bossy older sister, always taking over, questioning others' opinions.

I sent an email the next day apologizing about cutting her off. I thanked her for all she was doing, acknowledging how hard it is for all of us trying to find our way in helping Mum. She wrote back:

Lo,

I know you were reacting to the news – it's OK to vent on me!

I spoke to the oncologist this morning and will try to reach the Nurse Practitioner this afternoon to get more insight on the chemo side effects, etc.

R.

There will be angry words. Pain and sorrow can – and does -- bring out our ugly sides. Let it go. Let it go. Keep those you love close. Together you'll be stronger. And you're going to need all that strength in the coming weeks and months.

Caregiver Lesson #18

It's nice to be nice, especially when you feel like a bitch.

20 DO YOU HEAR THE PEEPERS?

"I think it's going to be tonight. It's my favorite night of the year. Do you think you'll be able to stay awake for it?" I ask Bette, acting like a five-year-old trying to talk her mother into going to a drive-in movie.

This annual rite means so much to me and I'd never shared it with Mum. The first and last time would be tonight. I hope she likes it as much as I do.

After finishing dinner, I brought our trays into the kitchen and cleaned up while Bette wrapped herself in a blanket close to the fire and turned on "Jeopardy." Dark already. I loaded up the dishwasher and took the garbage outside. I stopped just outside the door.

Could it be? I tossed the garbage into the composting bin and walked to the west side of the yard, closer to the marsh a few streets over.

Yes!

I rushed back in and helped Bette push her swollen feet into her green rubber garden shoes and get into her winter coat.

"I just knew it would be today," I said. "It's always the last week in March without fail."

I wrapped my arm in Mum's and out we went to the deck, arm in arm. It was so dark. Few stars and no moon. No lights on in any of the neighbors' houses. Today it reached 50-degrees, but most people are still in Florida.

Missing this.

"Do you hear them?" I asked. Gingerly we walked through the backyard, closer to the marsh.

Peep. Peep. Peep, sang the tree frog peepers in their song of spring joy. The Hallelujah chorus signals the Yuletide season. The Peepers are the official welcoming chorus of spring. Their high- pitched little voices tell us that the harshness and dark of the New England winter are over.

New beginnings and possibilities are coming. Rejoice. Be grateful.

Bette and I stand there listening. I know this will not be a joyful spring. The nurse's note this week said, "Declining rapidly."

But still, standing there with my Mum I sensed joy. Bette was always giving that to us, even when she had every excuse to be selfish. Like tonight.

We walked back into the house and cranked up the heat.

"It won't be long now," Bette said.

I hoped she meant the spring.

Caregiver Lesson #19

Celebrate peepers and any and all other little joys.

21 SMALL ESCAPES WITH EMMA AND DUSTIN

One of the worst things about dying is the boredom.

Bette gets up about the same time every day, showers, eats, watches a little TV, reads some.

Then most of the day is a crapshoot. Will she have any energy for anything? Or will the rest of the day be in bed, sleeping? Maybe strong enough for dinner. Maybe not.

"Dying is so boring, I feel like I'm going out of my mind, stuck in this house. Every day is the same," complains the usually non-complaining Bette.

The days have a rhythm but no pulse.

One Wednesday at noontime Bette calls up to me in the den. "Can you break free of your work for a couple of hours? Let's go to the movies. Come on, let's go right now before I lose my energy."

I hesitate, but we go.

We walk out of the bright, frigid March air into the dark Cineplex to escape for 92 minutes with the lovable Emma Thompson and Dustin Hoffman in an unlovable movie.

But we love it because it's broken the boredom. Bette's and mine.

Going to the movies made us feel, well, normal. We are a family of movie-goers, seeing all the good ones before Oscar night so we can really get into the show.

Emma and Dustin stroll around London, they and the city looking their very best. The banter is witty, though predictable, much like the plot. But who cares today? Bette and I are walking along the Thames with Emma and Dustin, crashing a glamorous wedding, rooting for our adorable underdogs, feeling the magic of people falling in love.

Pretty good for 92 un-boring minutes.

When Bette called up the stairs and said, "Let's go to the movies," I almost said, "Mum, that might be pushing it today. It might sap what little energy you have."

I almost tried to convince her to rest.

But then I remembered her boredom. Her lovely house has become her prison, where she stays every day for the duration, however long or short that may be.

When boredom hits, go to the movies. Go for a drive along favorite streets. Go for whatever your loved one can and wants to do at that moment.

Bust out of boredom even if it's for a little B-movie.

Caregiver Lesson #20

Beware the boredom. Bust out whenever and wherever possible.

22 WHAT'S YOUR PAUL NEWMAN SOLUTION?

I've always thought Paul Newman was a good actor, but I never felt the swooning sexual attraction that my mother and her friends had for him. Of course, they were Paul's contemporaries and knew him in the day – his and theirs.

I call him Paul, not Paul Newman, because I feel like I'm on a first name basis with him.

Not because I fell in love with those blue eyes or ever got the heartthrob thing – even when he starred with Robert Redford in "Butch Cassidy and the Sundance Kid." Not because he was so memorable in that first movie Bette let me stay up late to watch. (It was "The Silver Chalice" and all I could remember at age four was how bad an actor he seemed. The movie had props more fake than the ones we kids used out in the garage for our plays.)

No, I love Paul for his salad dressing. Not the Newman's Own Creamy Caesar with a drawing on the label of one of those Roman guys he played in that boring movie with the bad acting. The salad dressing I love Paul for is Newman's Own Olive Oil and Vinegar.

As caregivers, we are in charge of food, but thinking of what to make gets harder and harder the sicker and sicker the person gets. When sisters or Aunts come in to beef up the caregiver posse, the challenge of what to make for dinner magnifies.

But Paul saves me every time.

You see, if you pour Paul Newman's Own Olive Oil & Vinegar dressing on anything it goes from bland to good. Not great, but no one is expecting great in these circumstances.

Boil some Rigatoni, add cherry tomatoes, pitted Calamari olives and drench it with Paul Newman's Dressing. Cook that six- minute Orzo, add some basil, feta cheese, and leftover cherry tomatoes and drown it in Paul Newman's. Salad? Well that's a no- brainer. Marinating meat or chicken? Quick run out and buy several more bottles.

After one particularly stressful day, my sisters and I plopped ourselves on stools and draped our exhausted bodies over the kitchen island, reaching for chips and cold beers.

"What are we going to do about dinner," Nancy asked. "Should we call for pizza?"

"Nah," the rest of us said, "Not pizza. Isn't there anything left?"

We found a couple of cans of tuna fish, some limp lettuce, a tiny wedge of cheese of unknown variety – bland but no mold – and some frozen peas.

Renie started to open up a jar of mayonnaise for the tuna. The rest of us screamed, "No! Not mayonnaise."

We went to the pantry and found a fresh bottle of Paul Newman's. Dinner was delicious.

God bless Paul Newman. May his soul rest in peace knowing that his generosity lives on, helping people in ways he never imagined.

Caregiver Lesson #21

Steal this Paul Newman's all-purpose cooking secret.

23 MANAGING VISITS: TIME'S UP, SISTER

Some days dying people can handle visits, other days they're just too weak and tired. We're learning that the on-duty caregiver needs to politely police visits.

This means knowing when to say, "Not today." Or being clear on the best time to visit and how long the visit should last.

Yesterday my mother's friend Barbara called to see if she could come over for "cocktail hour" – Bette is usually up from 5-7:30 p.m. having a martini and dinner. Bette shook her head OK while I was on the phone with Barbara; I told Barbara an hour was too much, but 20 minutes would be just fine.

A related skill is learning how to wrap up the visit, giving the signal that it's time to go.

We find that Bette wants to be available to people who care so much about her. We also find that she overextends herself and appreciates someone else doing the polite policing.

The three questions we ask her about visitors:

1. So -and-so wants to stop by today. Are you up for it? (Yes/No) (Note people with terminal cancer have up days and down days. It's almost impossible to plan visits in advance, as the person can't predict how he

or she will be feeling. Don't be offended if people tell you that they can't plan ahead and to please call on the day you'd like to visit.)

2. Should we suggest 10 a.m. - noon or 5-6 p.m.? (Times she generally feels OK)

3. What do you think – is this a 15, 30 or 45-minute visit?

At first, it feels awkward to have to "close out" visits. Bette, such a welcoming hostess, never ever lets company feel like they are overstaying their welcome. But after some visits she says, "I just can't keep this up."

The on-duty caregiver has to take on the role of timekeeper, graciously (and sometimes not so graciously) telling visitors that "Time's up." Sometimes I feel like a female prison warden in a bad B movie. "Move it along now, sister. Can't you see that visiting hours are over?"

As bad as I feel kicking people out, I know Bette would feel worse struggling to keep her "I'm not that sick yet" game face on.

Caregiver Lesson #22

Set strict time limits for visitors.

24 DYING TO HELP: ASSIGN PEOPLE CHORES

Everyone wants to help, but most don't know what to do. They feel bad sitting by passively. We, the immediate caregivers, shouldn't try to do everything. More importantly, we have to help others contribute.

One way to do this is to figure out what people are good at, and feel comfortable doing, and ask them to do those things.

My brother David, for example, is a hard-working guy of few words. He's not good sitting around and "visiting." We ask him to drive people places, like driving our sister Susan the two hours from the Cape to the Providence airport.

Jim, our other brother, has been getting Mum's house ready for spring, staining the deck, fixing screens, bringing out some summer furniture. Susan, while up here from North Carolina, cleaned inside and out.

We asked Lew, Mum's brother, to get the car fixed and figure out things with the auto body shop and the insurance company.

People really are dying to help. If the head honcho caregivers step back for a minute, you can figure out all kinds of small but helpful ways for people to pitch in. The more people are involved the more the positive juju grows all around.

Caregiver Lesson #23

Assign people chores they're good at.

25 FIVE THINGS THAT REALLY PISS OFF CAREGIVERS

Some days you just have to rant to stay sane. Or keep a "what really pisses me off" list. Here are five small things that have made me crazy.

1. *Golf priorities*: When people keep saying, "Call me if there's anything I can ever do." One day you call and ask for a ride to the bus and the person says he can't help because he's playing golf.   We're exhausted here and need help, but golf comes first?

2. *Pollen excuses:* When the night hospice nurse, who you've called because things are not going well, tells you that the ill person's hacking cough could very well be because of "all the pollen in the air." The nurse comes back a week later and again reminds you that a lot of people are having problems with allergies. Er, hello, my mother has stage IV LUNG cancer. I'm no oncologist but something tells me that cancer in the lungs may have much more to do with the cough than pollen.

3. *Way overstaying a visit:* When you tell people who beg to come for a visit that the ill person is so weak that any visitors will make her sicker. After more pleading, you relent, remind the person to keep it short, and then they hang around for two hours, at which point you need to be curt, which creates more stress and this kind of stress is about the last thing that a harried caregiver can take.

4. *That's $3.99:* When a family friend asks if they can pick up anything at the grocery store for you. You ask for some orange juice. When they drop off the juice, they give you the receipt for $3.99. Come on, you

can't treat a dying friend to $3.99 juice? That's not being penurious, that's just bad manners.

5. *Losing it*: When you open an obscure kitchen cabinet looking for the blender and find a Tupperware container with leftover chicken cutlets from two weeks ago. Worse than the stench, is that you might be losing it amid the stress. What other stupid things might I have done lately?

Caregiver Lesson #24

Keep a "what pisses me off" list. But never share it. (Review lesson #18 again.)

26 LOVE THAT SICK HUMOR

When half your head is scalped from neurosurgery, you've been told that your stage IV cancer has spread like wildfire and your days are numbered, sometimes the best thing to do is tell sick jokes.

We come from a family that loves sick jokes. They make us laugh, they tell lessons, and they help us talk about difficult things. Needless to say, sick humor is part of our noodle as we try to stay afloat.

When people see , they are shocked at how different she looks, and she can see that shock in their faces. She can deal with that.

What's harder to deal with is when people say, "You look good."

When Bette hears this, she brings up one of her deceased husband's favorite jokes.

"You know what they say. There are three stages of life. Youth, middle age, and 'you look good.'"

This morning two trucks pulled up to the house behind Bette's and a crew of six strapping young guys start pulling off shingles and re-roofing the summer cottage. Oh, oh, I thought, thinking of one of our family's favorite jokes, I hope this isn't a sign that Bette's going to be on the roof soon.

The joke goes like this:

A man goes on vacation and leaves his dog with his brother. The first night away he calls his brother to ask about his dog.

"Hi, how is my little Spot doing?" asks the vacationing brother.

"Your dog died," says his brother.

"What?!!!," screams the other brother. "You're not supposed to just come out and tell me like that. The first night I call you're supposed to say my dog is stuck on the roof. The next time I call you're supposed to tell me that the dog fell off the roof. The third night I call you tell me that the dog died. Got it?"

"Got it."

"Okay, good," says the brother on vacation. "I'll call you tomorrow to check in."

The next day he calls and asks his brother, "So how is everything going?"

"Good. The weather is nice, sunny and warm, not too hot, not too cold." says his brother, making pleasant chitchat.

"Great, glad to hear it. And how is mom?"

"She's on the roof."

I peek into Bette's room. No, she won't be on the roof today.

Caregiver Lesson #25

Tell lots of sick jokes. Even at inappropriate times. Especially at inappropriate times.

27 RESPECTING OTHERWORLDLY SIGNS

Part of helping people with this dying process is shutting up and listening. And respecting dreams, signs, and, who knows, maybe some sort of spirit guides hovering around.

The "who knows" part is important. I've never been one of those touchy-feely, new age kind of people. Logic has been my North Star. But when the dying person shares special dreams or signs, we must put aside our biases, and honor those signs. This is their journey and we're here to help, not judge.

Bette wanted to share a story, but then stopped and said, "Oh, it's probably foolishness. I'm too embarrassed to talk about it."

But clearly, she wanted to talk about it.

"The night your father died I felt someone put an arm around my shoulder and give me a hug. I felt the warmth of that arm. It wasn't like a dream. Today when I was napping that same arm hugged me three times.   Now I don't feel as scared about what's going to happen. I know I'm dying and it's OK."

And I realized by listening respectfully I made it more OK.

Caregiver Lesson #26

Shut up and listen.

28 FOUL MOODS

I'm sitting here on Cape Cod and the rain is blowing sideways, straight ways and relentlessly. It's May but the day is dark and so is Bette's mood. Foul all around. And not nice foul, like foul balls in Fenway Park on a hot summer night.

The bickering during the last 24 hours has been proportionate to what I see as the evil cancer soldiers marching more aggressively through Bette's body, looking for new places to set camp and make a new mess. The more territory they claim this week, the more irritated she becomes. Rightly so. But still...

Though she can barely stay awake more than a few hours and the cancer has spread to her brain (again) Bette boldly stated yesterday that she wanted to see the oncologist and make sure it was OK to start driving.

"Drive?" I asked incredulously. "How could you even think about that? Look at the state you're in. You could hurt someone driving."

"I don't want to discuss it with you. But I am going to talk to the doctor about it. Now call the auto repair shop and get the car back today."

"Why today? I have my car."

"I want the car and I want to see the doctor about driving." Oy.

Later it was about the trash.

"Why are you using those trash bags," asked Bette. "Just use these plastic grocery bags."

"But those are too small. They don't hold enough and they're flimsy," I shot back.

"You're being ridiculous. Use these."

Today Bette is laid low, unable to do much at all but sleep. The foul mood has ebbed. I suppose yesterday's irritation was all about fighting the new cancer soldiers. Today she's accepting them.

It's still raining.

Caregiver Lesson #27

Let foul moods blow themselves out.

29 THE WISE WOMAN WORRIER GOES BANANAS

Our little Cape house on the dead-end street was quiet. The television in Bette's room automatically turns off at 10 p.m. She usually falls asleep at 8 p.m. but likes the TV on in the room. Strange company, but, hey, whatever works when you're dying.

I had gone upstairs to the den after Mum settled in after dinner and turned on the other TV, snuggling into the plaid pullout couch and wrapping myself up in the cranberry afghan my grandmother had made years ago.

Ah, eureka! Thursday night and a new episode of my favorite series, one of life's small pleasures living at my mother's house while my family was in their own orbit back in Rhode Island.

After the silly sitcom it was time for the routine – a little flossing, brushing the teeth, scrubbing the face and then lathering on the super-thick Wise Woman Goddess nighttime face lotion for "mature women."

Maybe at last I'd act mature, like Audrey Hepburn. Elegant. Soft spoken. Manicured. As flawless in beauty and social skills as Audrey's skin.

But wait, is that the phone ringing? No one calls the house at 11 p.m.

"Is this Elizabeth Kelly?"

"No, this is her daughter. May I help you?"

"Well, Mrs. Kelly was here for blood tests earlier today."

"Yes, and…" I quickly replied, clearly losing Audrey's coolness.

"Well, I'm sorry to disturb you so late but I'm required by law to call because Mrs. Kelly's potassium level is dangerously low. It's below 2.5. We'll also be calling her doctor."

"So, exactly does this mean. I mean, what should I being doing?" I asked.

"Well," the lab doctor said, "Call her doctor first thing in the morning. And give her some bananas as soon as you can to get the potassium levels up. The doctor will also likely prescribe medication. Sorry to have to have had to call you so late."

Geez, Louise, I thought hanging up. Now what? I went online and Googled "low potassium."

Up it came. "When the potassium level drops to less than2.5mEq/L then the condition is life threatening and in need of emergency medical attention. The effects of low potassium in the body is the formation of a potentially fatal state called "hypokalemia."

Hypokalemia? Fatal? Jesus, I thought. What if she dies of this instead of the cancer?

I went downstairs and tiptoed into Bette's bedroom. No sound, no movement. Oh, dear God. I walked closer and put my face down close to hers.

Yes! She's breathing!

Then I went into the kitchen and got two yellowy-green bananas and went back into her bedroom. Medicine time.

I looked at my mother's face. She looked so restful. Almost young. Could it be possible that you lose all your wrinkles when you have terminal cancer? She was lovely in a way I had never seen before. Or maybe it was how the streetlight was shining through the peach-colored bedroom curtains.

"Or maybe," said the wise woman goddess voice in my head, the Audrey Hepburn mature woman, "she's finally having a good night's sleep for the first time since the brain surgery. The medicine is making the potassium levels low, but the sleep is making her beautiful."

"You're right, wise woman," I said, walking back to the kitchen and tossing the bananas on the counter. "Let Bette sleep."

Back upstairs I went, turning down the thermostat to 63 degrees, climbing into bed while trying to push Bobby McFerrin's "Don't Worry, Be Happy" song out of my head.

I was happy that Bette was sleeping soundly. But I worried all night. It's part of what we caregivers do. You get really good as the nighttime Wise Woman Goddess of Worry, watching over the sick, the unknown, the 2.5 potassium levels.

And that's why I highly recommend that you stock up on extra jars of the Wise Woman Goddess night cream. Maybe even wear it during the day.

Caregiver Lesson #28

Celebrate that you are becoming a wise woman worrier, an honor earned only by caring so selflessly for someone so ill.

30 HESITATING ON HOSP-ICE

People wait too long to bring in hospice.

Although hospice can provide care over the last six months of a person's life, studies show that the median length of time most people are enrolled in hospice is only 26 days; 33 percent of hospice patients are enrolled in the last seven days of life, and 10 percent are enrolled in the last 24 hours.

One reason I guess is that hospice means admitting that you're very sick, almost at the end of the line.

I also think it's the word itself. Hosp-ice.

"Hosp" to me says hospital – illness, sterile environments, nurses, doctors and aides you don't know, loss of freedom, sleeping in an institutional bed with institutional sheets, bland food, pillows that make your neck ache, visiting hours, orders, tests, new pills. And, worst of all, sharing a room with a stranger and the stranger's family. All at a time when you are so, so sick.

The other part of the word is "ice." Another not pleasant association when you're dying. Putting someone on ice means keeping them intact until the out-of-town family members can get home for the funeral. Or it conjures up mobster movies where the Capo gives the order to ice the snitch.

No, who wants to sign up earlier than possible to be hosp iced.

Bette certainly resisted.

"I'm just not ready for that. Now I don't want to talk about it anymore," she stated.

(Cue the music again, "You've got the power.")

I let her command sink into the room. I turn on the gas fireplace and tuck the afghan around her legs as she sits in her wing chair.

"Want a cup of tea?" I ask.

"Yes, that would be nice. I just can't get warm. It's so cold this spring. You'd think we'd get one or two warm days by now."

I make the tea and as we sit sipping it, I say, "You know Mum, you might not be ready for hospice. But maybe this is a good time to get all the paperwork and administrative stuff done while you're feeling OK. You don't have to commit to the care part until you want. But it would be easier for you to handle the paperwork with hospice than me."

My mother, a former government administrator, office manager and secretary extraordinaire, knew that no one was as efficient and organized as she. And she wanted to be in charge of her situation as long as possible.

"I'll think about it," she said.

I went upstairs to the den to work. When I came downstairs two hours later the phone was on the table by her chair, as was her calendar.

"They're coming tomorrow at 9 a.m.," she said.

"Who?"

"The hospice people," said Bette. "I think you're right. I need to get all the administrative things done."

The hospice admissions people came the next day to do the paperwork. The day after that the hospice nurse assigned to Bette came for an evaluation and get-to-know chat. The nurse also gave us "the box" and told us to keep it in the refrigerator so we would always know where to find the medication and supplies we were going to need down the line.

Three days later we were down the line. The first crisis hit.

 "Good thing I made the decision to sign up with hospice," said a tired Bette.

Good thing indeed Mum.

PS – Hospice care is nothing like hosp-ice. Maybe this warm, caring type of medical service needs a name makeover, something akin to what Gentle Giant has done to change the perception of moving companies.

Caregiver Lesson #29

Bring hospice into your lives sooner than you think you need them. Everything gets easier even as it gets harder.

31 NEIN ON 911

One of the deals with hospice is that you're never to call 911.

That was like telling me that I had to do a circus high wire act, my first ever, with no safety net.

"If something happens," explained the hospice nurse, give your mother up to this amount of the morphine from the bottle in the box in the refrigerator. Then call us. Someone is always available."

I see. Hospice personnel are the spotters who catch you because there's no net.

The nurse was originally from Liverpool, England and had a lyrical Irish accent. ("Half of Liverpool is from Ireland, so we all sound Irish," she once told me.) Despite her calm instructions and reassuring words, eliminating 911 was scary.

911 is always there for us. Heart attacks. Accidents. Falls. Bizarre situations with no explanation. Don't worry, 911 is on its way, ready to administer emergency treatment, reassure frightened relatives and neighbors and whisk the sick, the injured, the stunned to the closest hospital emergency room.

We teach our children at a young age to dial 9-1-1. They learn these three numbers before their own phone number.

"Now what do you do if something happens?" we drill them.

"Call 9-1-1."

"Very good. Give mummy a big hug."

Now my 'mummy' needs much more than a hug. She needs new lungs un-touched by cancer cells. A brain free of malignant tumors floating this way and that, one day obstructing her ability to read, the next day snuffing out her memory.

"Remember now, no 911," repeats the hospice nurse. "Tell the others who will be caring for your mother, too. Here's a magnet to put on the refrigerator as a reminder."

Every time I go to the fridge and see the magnet, I feel a sense of responsibility that is new and different, overwhelming really. As a mother with my own child I could always call 911 or call my mother if something bad happened.

Now I cannot call 911. Nor can I call my own mother. For now, I am the one she must call.

No safety nets. No clue of how bad it might get.

Caregiver Lesson #30

When the safety nets are gone, count on your spotters.

32 SCARED SHITLESS, AND FINDING GRACE

Now that's a terrible heading for this story. (The first part, anyway.) Maybe I should have titled it, "acute stress attack" or "physiology and psychology of the stress response." Whatever you call it, when the dying person you love goes into their first dangerous "oh-my-God-I-can't-breathe" attack, you, the caregiver, are put to The First Big Test.

(Mmm, maybe that's a better title).

Bette was turning red then purple as she coughed and tried to get a breath. I ran to the refrigerator and opened the morphine that hospice had provided, figuring out how to put the plunger in, turn the bottle upside down, take the plunger out to the right dose, and oh dear God, hope that I wouldn't spill the morphine all over the place because we're probably going to need much more of this drug.

Bette was trying to give instructions but couldn't talk for lack of air. I squeezed the morphine under her tongue. She gagged at the taste, still fighting for air. I propped some pillows and helped her sit up, hoping that position would make her more comfortable. Then I called hospice, left a message, and got Bette a little cranberry juice to help her overcome the taste of the morphine.

Through it all, I stayed calm, talked slowly and reassured Bette that she'd be just fine once the drug kicked in. I sat on her bed a while as she settled, shaken but able to breath.

Now anyone who knows me knows that I tend to be hyper, overly excited and occasionally manic when I'm stressed. Not today, though I felt scared through my whole being. Scared shitless as hardcore Bostonians would say.

But I also felt a spiritual otherness, being able to love Bette by helping and in doing so finding grace.

Caregiver Lesson #31

The more frightening the situation, the calmer you must be. It is in the calmness that you will find grace, a gift bestowed upon caregivers to help us get through all of this.

33 DON'T FORGET YOUR KIDS

I'm home for the weekend, cleaning my house. My husband is at work, my 14-year-old son Ian is at a friend's.

This morning I asked Ian how he is, trying to catch up on what's happening at school, how he's feeling about his grandmother, and just how he is.

"I'm good, Mum. School is fine. Don't worry about me. You do know you worry and nag too much, don't you?"

I give him a hug that he half reciprocates, stepping closer to me and putting his arms around me, but not letting his hands touch my back for more than a millisecond.

"Mum, no more public displays of affection. I'm a teenager."

"Public displays? We're in our own kitchen."

"You know what I mean, Mum."

"Are you sure you're OK about Nanie? You're not talking much about it."

"Mum, I'm fine. Stop worrying so much."

The house is quiet, and I walk from room to room, spying what's been happening while I'm at my mother's during the week. I sort the bills, fold two baskets of laundry. Check what's in the refrigerator and find big Tupperware containers of spaghetti and meatballs. Gosh, their diet while I'm away during the week is pretty boring.

I walk into the mess that is a 14-year-old's room and find school papers strewn over what allegedly is a desk. It looks more like a trash heap. There are candy wrappers from the stash of Halloween candy that I know Ian keeps somewhere in this room. Magazines. Last year's class yearbook. Three-ring binders that have never been used. Pencils that need to be sharpened. Scraps of paper with passwords and email addresses scribbled on them.

I look through the papers piled on the desk and find poems, written for English class. I pull them out, read them, and then sit on the floor.

"Oh God. This is not good. Please tell me he's OK."

The poems are dark, all about death. Did I read somewhere that if a teenager obsesses about death you should get immediate psychiatric attention? Is Ian in trouble?   He seems so sweet and positive and funny. But this stash of poems is alarming.

I read the last one and realize that he has been paying attention when we've talked at dinner about the stages of death. Though I'm calmly panicked, I realize that this teenager, so reluctant to display affection, is torn up about his grandmother.

I wish boys would talk more.

Forget to Remember

By Ian Matta

Every morning,

Not knowing if she will wake up.

Day by day she's getting pulled away. Farther and farther into darkness. Denial is the only thing

That can comfort her.

Right after anger, acceptance,

And Death.

If only there was a way

To forget to remember

This is not happening.

Caregiver Lesson #32

Though consumed with caregiving, find time for the quiet bystanders who may need you too.

34 RRRTEO: THE LAST WORD

Scrabble in our family is more than a pastime. It's a social ritual, an escape, and sometimes a ruthless, competitive sport.

I set up the Scrabble game, trying to position the board on an ottoman in front of Bette's chair as she is too weak to sit at a table. The first bad sign started before the game began. Bette kept dropping the tiles on the floor, not being able to place them on the letter tray. I helped her get them settled. She had drawn an "E" and I an "M," so she went first.

It took her a long time to make a word. "What's wrong with my brain," she kept saying in frustration.

"Maybe we shouldn't play today. It's afternoon and you're usually really tired around this time. Why push it," I offered.

"No, I am going to do this. I need to do this," Bette stated. After about 10 minutes, she made her word: RRRTOE.

"Um, Mum, what's that word?"

"It's reroute. It is, isn't it? , what's happening to me?"

Bette started to get agitated and frightened. The cancer in her brain was going haywire in new ways.

I put the game away, got her some anti-anxiety medicine and we sat quietly. No spoken words help at moments like this. We both knew this was bad, a new symptom messing with her mind. After a few minutes I turned on "Oprah," which was part of the afternoon routine. We didn't watch the program as much as let it calm down the unsettling recognition that terminal cancer wreaks havoc. It's both unpredictable and unkind.

That night I lay in bed thinking about REROUTE, the word Bette had wanted to make. Her life was being rerouted and she didn't like where it was going. In her weak state she couldn't scream, pound a wall or run out of the house to take out her anger on the world and this terminal illness. But she could mangle the word that was scrabbling her life.

I was helpless to help.

Caregiver Lesson #33

Some days nothing will make sense.

35 BIG 'C' AND SMALL 'C' COURAGE

Courage is such a big word, reserved for heroes who pull people from burning buildings, save little children from drowning, rescue coal miners stuck in the shaft.

Courage is for death-defying feats. Tiptoeing onto the thin ice, sliding the ladder out to the open water, calmly coaching the young boy on how to grab on. The fireman never loses concentration.

"Just grab on and you'll be OK. Yes, son, you're going to be all right. Be strong now, be strong. Here comes the ladder. Reach up. Grab the end. A little closer. You're almost there, almost there. It's going to be OK. I have you. I have you."

Then screams of victory. Women and men crying. Dogs barking. The parents heaving, gulping frigid sobs as the EMTs wrap the boy in a sliver space blanket, lift him in their arms and run to the ambulance.

The courageous fireman puts the ladder back on the side of the truck. His buddies slap him on the back. They high-five.

Oh Courage, you strong savior. You're Courage with a capital "C."

The day-in, day-out caring for someone who is sick is courage, too, but small "c" courage. There's no glamour. No big momentous event. No crowds cheering you on, slapping you on the back after you help the person you love inch his or her way into the bathroom at 3 a.m. Waiting outside the bathroom door, ready to help the person slowly, slowly get back into bed.

This courage won't make the six o'clock news. It won't win special awards or recognition. It won't even deserve a conversation when people check in with you tomorrow.

"How is she doing? Anything new or unusual?" they call and ask.

 "No, everything is about the same," you say.

They don't know about small "c" courage. The courage not to complain, feel badly for yourself that you're stuck sleeping on the couch so that you can jump up at 3 a.m. for bathroom duty. Courage not to cry in front of the sick person the next day because you're so tired that all you want to do is sleep in a bed, without being on call.

This small "c" courage is Love. Love with a capital "L."

Caregiver Lesson #34

The courage from this experience will empower you to do anything when life shifts "back to normal."

36 SHARE EVERYTHING

Family and friends who can't be with the ill person worry, feel guilty, and lose concentration during their workdays wondering what's going on today.

Sometimes I don't want to add to these anxieties or worry anyone needlessly as I don't really know what's going to happen one day to the next. But I've found that my sisters and brothers, aunts and uncles, feel better knowing the details than not knowing.

When on chief honcho caregiver duty, I send daily emails to the rest of the tribe. One brother is Luddite and doesn't use email, but my other brother calls to keep him posted.

What may seem like "over-communication" can also help the caregiver on duty to be able to share a jumble of emotions and thoughts, and it helps whoever is next on duty know what they're walking into. Here are some examples:

Hi Nance,

Mom is in good spirits this morning. Mood is positive. Eyes bright. Constipation under control. And she had a nice shower. Hope you can enjoy today, knowing Mum is OK and FINALLY spring is here.

Lois

Lois:

I cannot tell you how much I appreciate this message. When I saw your name, my heart raced and sank. I will be coming Friday. Thanks again.

Nancy

Hi all:

I have to share the end of the day, work backwards and then fill you in on what we need to do for Mum.

Mum, wobbly on her feet tonight but insisting that she make her own martini, is standing pouring the vodka onto the counter, missing the shot glass by half an inch. The vodka is everywhere, until I take it out of her hands. "Oh, I'm losing my mind again. Can't find words or put things in a glass."

Earlier in the day Mum had a really sudden, severe coughing attack where she couldn't get her breath. I bumbled around, got the morphine into her and she settled down, then had horrific stomach pains. Hospice nurse came, said the stomach pains were probably from the strain from coughing.

Back up a day. I'm cleaning up after supper and find Mum on the floor, having lost her balance after getting up from her chair.

The cancer soldiers are claiming territory in her body, meaning someone needs to be with Mum all the time – even if she tells you she's fine, do not leave until the next caregiver comes on duty. These new symptoms seem to sneak up and wreak havoc. Do not accept, "I'm fine." She isn't.

Most of all, be patient. Her mind is slipping. She's having a hard time finding words, confuses people and stories. She wants to be useful, but shouldn't be trying to cook, pour hot water – or even juice (or vodka). I told her, with the support of the hospice nurse, that she should let us to do these tasks so she can conserve energy, making sure she can do essentials, like bathing without help.

So, it's a tricky balance, not smothering her, but making sure she's OK. The worst would be for her to fall and break something.

Some practical things:

Ativan is like a miracle drug; she needs to take it regularly. When in doubt, give her an Ativan.

The morphine is by the side of her bed. If she needs it, fill the little plunger up to 5 (about a quarter) and put it under her tongue. Make sure there's cranberry juice ready to chase the awful morphine taste.

If she needs the morphine, also give her an Ativan at the same time, per hospice nurse.

The tel # for hospice is on a magnet on the 'fridge; ask them to page her nurse Claire.

Never, ever call 911. Call hospice. Even when you're scared shitless, like I was today.

Claire, the nurse, will be back on Tues. at 10, with a new supply of drugs.

Mom's not on the roof but it feels like she's on the ladder.

My love, Lois

Caregiver Lesson #35

Over-communicate.

37 DOUBT IS A DEVIL

"I've always believed that there is something after this life. Now I don't know. And it's making me scared," said Bette.

"When living my life, I just accepted religious beliefs about heaven, everlasting souls, the "white light," joining loved ones who have died before us," mused Bette.

Like saying prayers, these beliefs are ingrained from a lifetime of worship, yet rarely do we think about the words behind the prayers or interrogate the meaning of the beliefs.

But when you know you're going to die soon you think about these concepts – and many are hard to believe. There's no proof, after all. Just conjecture. Is anyone really sure that Jesus, Mohammad, Buddha, Joseph Smith, Jr., Confucius, Zoroaster or any other holy men had the inside skinny on what really happens after you die?

Bette talked about this fear and her doubts last night, coming to no conclusions, simply acknowledging that as the cancer weakens her body, so does her belief about afterlife.

Then today the retired Monsignor of her church, who she traveled with, who helped her through her grief after my father died, and who she hasn't talked with since his retirement a few years ago, called out of the blue.

"I heard you were sick," he said. "You must be scared."

"I am,' she said.

"It's going to be alright. You'll be fine," he said.

Monsignor Tosti's call comforted Bette and provided much needed reassurance that whatever happens, she will be fine. It didn't resolve her doubts about belief, but it did strengthen her faith.

Caregiver Lesson #36

Be open to faith.

38 MORE THANKFULNESS, LESS HOPE

When it comes to dying, people want you to be hopeful. To talk about possibilities, about people who lived much longer than doctors predicted, about miracles.

When I've had to have frank sit-downs with family and Bette's friends to explain her situation, people listen as I cut through all the niceties and tell them that Bette does not have long to live.

I also tell them that she's OK with dying and needs them to be OK with it too. She's so thankful for the life she's had – and for all that they've been in her life.

"You're being awfully negative," comes the reply. "You need to have hope and be more positive."

If this happened once, I'd overlook it. But there's a pattern.

Why can't people celebrate thankfulness? Why is that virtue so overlooked when it comes to dying? What happened to the mantras, "Be thankful for what you have" and "Be thankful for every day?" "Make a list of what you want your obituary to read so you can be thankful that you lived the life you wanted."

When people are dying hope is overrated, and thankfulness is the goddess to worship. How great is it when you're dying to be able to look back on your life and say, "I am so very thankful." How joyful is it to hear someone express their thankfulness, and for your part in it?

It's more than joyful. It's inspiring.

And that's far more powerful than empty hope.

Caregiver Lesson #37

Practice gratitude. This lifts your spirits and those around you.

39 BODILY MALFUNCTIONS AND OTHER SHIT

I can't write about this. You see, as a caregiver I could not help when Bette decided to clean herself out so there would be no ugly bowel related messes.

She knew that she was going down fast and wanted to take charge of making sure that nothing would be left when she no longer had the strength to get to the bathroom.

She was intent on making sure that she – and we – would suffer no greater indignities than necessary.

I knew I should just get over it and be able to help her into the bathroom after all those laxatives, scrub the toilet bowl and help her shower and clean up.

I couldn't. I felt the bile creep up into my throat. My sisters and aunt looked at me and said, "Don't worry about it. We'll do it."

I felt so guilty. Here were these courageous women just moving in and doing what had to be done. No thinking. No self- absorption about what they were feeling. Just get the job done. There, now that's over. Let's go for a walk and forget about it.

In this adventure there will be things you just can't do. It's OK. Know your limits and call in those people – family and friends or paid assistance – who can do it.

Then make those angels a special meal or buy them their favorite dessert or let them watch whatever they want on the television. Honor them for being able to do what they do. Even if you cannot. Especially because you cannot.

And know that it's OK that you can't do everything.

Caregiver Lesson #38

Know your limits. Ask for help.

40 MORPHINE MORAL DILEMMAS

"I want you to give me some special help at the end," says Bette.

"What do you mean by 'special help,' Mum?"

"You know what I'm talking about," insists Bette.

"Mum, I don't."

"I did it for Dad at the end, you know. "

I didn't know what she did for my father or what she was talking about.

"I want you to give me a lot of morphine, so much that it will help me go faster," Bette says.

"Mum, we can't do that. It's against the law."

"I will need it, and no one needs to know except for you and maybe Nancy. That's what I want. At the end things need to be speeded up," she matter-of-factly explained. "So, let's not talk about it anymore. Just promise me that you'll help me go quickly."

For weeks I thought about this request, more of an instruction really. Would it be so bad to double, triple, quadruple the morphine?

When someone's so close to death it's not that you're killing them, just providing medication and comfort, right? No one would ever have to know.

One day after Bette lost consciousness, only occasionally opening her eyes but not recognizing us, I sat with my sister at the kitchen island drinking coffee and sharing the crossword puzzle.

"You know what Mum wants us to do, don't you?" I said.

"No, what?"

"Give her an overdose of morphine to help her go faster."

"That doesn't surprise me," said Nancy. "It would be so much easier for her. She's suffering so much."

"Should we?" I wondered out loud.

I filled in a couple of more answers to the crossword puzzle and slid it over to Nancy to see if she could fill in any. We let the question softly boomerang around the quiet house.

Later that morning Sister, a retired nun and friend of my mother came to visit. My mother had always liked Sister because she is so down to earth, positive and appreciates a good joke. Even the off-colored ones.

Before going into the bedroom, she asked, "How is she?" "Not good, Sister, not good at all."

Sister went in and sat on the dining room chair that we had put by Mum's bedside. She held Bette's hand for a while, and when she came out of the bedroom she was crying.

"This is so difficult to see," she said and hugged me hard. We cried and quickly pulled ourselves back together.

"You know, Sister," I blurted. "Bette asked us to help her go faster when she got to this point."

"We have to leave her in God's hands," Sister said. Not in a preachy way, just in a matter of fact way that held no judgment, like "we have to fill the bird feeder before the storm."

Later the hospice nurse came and said we should feel comfortable upping the morphine dosage. We went to the max, but no further.

Our only illegal drug-taking was occasionally sneaking some of Bette's Ativan anti-anxiety pills and taking them ourselves. They calmed us down as we measured the morphine plunger and disobeyed our mother.

Caregiver Lesson #39

Don't break the law – no matter what your mother tells you to do.

41 GRAB THE FURLOUGH

I am no longer the dingbat Private Judy Benjamin. I am a caregiver Navy Seal, having gone through ordeals that I never expected I could survive. Here I am, on the front lines, ready, waiting. Bring it on, I can handle it. Hoo-yah.

Someone suggests that maybe I should go home to my family for a couple of days. Or get in the car and drive down out to the National Seashore for a little break.

How can I go off duty?

I've got an acute sense of those cancer guerilla warfare types hiding in the bush. I know the signs of impending danger and how to protect my mother. I know how to give her the morphine and crushed up Ativan so she can swallow it. I'm skilled at keeping well- meaning visitors at bay. And cooking? I can make dinner with one bottle of Paul Newman's Oil & Vinegar and any other ingredient you throw at me.

The other worry: what if after all this Mum dies while I'm off duty?

The Clash "Should I Stay or Go Now" song rings in my head. The repressed shrew inside my head wants to unleash anger that may harm innocent bystanders.

Then a more mature Private Benjamin whispers in my ear, "Pull yourself together and act like the disciplined Navy Seal that you are."

I take the furlough.

Caregiver Lesson #40

Get off the base for R&R before you violate lesson #18.

42 HURRY UP AND DIE

Here's the dirty little secret we caregivers share. A shameful secret that few talk about.

As the end nears you start wishing the person you love so much would hurry up and die.

I mean how much more can anyone take. The person you love is no longer conscious much of the day, if at all. The day is one of tedious tasks – morphine every hour, sponging Mum's body, turning her gently to avoid bed sores – and quietly sitting holding Mum's hand. Bette moans and stiffens further into a fetal position, with her right hand becoming more permanently bent, as if her human hand was turning into a puppy paw, asking for a treat.

If she were asking for a treat, I imagine her saying, "Oh, please dear God, take me. I want to go quickly and with dignity. These daughters of mine now have to put those horrible adult diapers on me. Such humiliation. Please, I'm begging, take me and spare them having to do this. I don't want them to remember me this way."

But Bette no longer talks. She just moans and whimpers.

"Is she in pain," callers ask.

As the morphine cocktail – four-fifths morphine, one-fifth cranberry juice to cut the horrific taste – dribbles from her mouth, I worry that nothing is getting into her system and, yes, there is pain. Hospice says it's too late for an IV drip; Bette's veins probably wouldn't take it.

It's 9 a.m., noon, 3 p.m., dinner time, 9, 11, two in the morning, four in the morning; the sun is coming up, coffee time, breakfast. More morphine. Turn Bette over and sponge bathe her. Change the sheets. Cut a clean nightgown up the back so we can more easily get it over her head without causing her too much pain.

More moans. Not wimpy moans like a puppy with its cute paw raised for a treat, but an old dog's moans, a dog who needs to be put down because he can no longer make it outside to pee. His food goes through him and comes out like sludge. He needs to be carried up the stairs at night, though he mostly stays on newspaper on the kitchen floor.

"Please God, make her die. How many more days must she suffer? When does it all end so we can live again? Go to work, sleep all night, be in our own beds?

"Damn, stop it. That's selfish," we remind ourselves. Shame. Shame. Shame.

A close friend calls and we remember that while her husband was dying, she planned a three-week vacation to Hawaii. We were appalled. "How selfish," we gossiped.

Now we know how beat caregivers become. How much you need something to look forward to. Something where you can plan, control, mark the calendar dates with certainty.

At the end, I feel like a watcher, not a giver. I am powerless at a time when the best mother in the world lays dying, gurgling and choking on the fluid in her lungs. But not the morphine she so needs.

Please God, hurry up and make Mum die.

Caregiver Lesson #41

Wishing for death is not selfish nor something to feel guilty about. It is your compassion showing, and that's a good thing.

43 TEND TO THE FINAL DETAILS

Bette lays in her bed, curled up, unconscious. Mostly the room is quiet. I hear her occasionally cough and gurgle the fluid that is filling her lungs and ending her life.

I hear lawnmowers and weed-whackers and remember that people are getting their houses ready for summer.

Memorial Day, the long weekend where summer officially begins for New Englanders, is almost here. For so many years we've had a big party here, kids sleeping on air mattresses on floors, adult kids vying for the beds, Bette making her delicious potato salad with just a touch of sugar, lines for the outdoor shower, sandy sandals lined up on the deck, sweatshirts all over the house. Not this year.

The phone rings asking whether my sisters or I want to go to a surprise birthday party tonight for Bette's brother, up at the Inn on the beach.

"No, we say. "Not now."

I lay on the couch outside Mum's room and read, waiting for the stove timer to buzz, reminding me it's time to give her more morphine. I'm only vertical when I need to tend to Bette. All energy has vaporized.

Then there are new noises. Down the stairs march my sisters, dressed, makeup on, and with determined looks in their eyes. They are on a mission.

"What's going on," I ask, looking up from my couch cocoon.

"We're going to the funeral home, the church, the florist, and the caterer," they say. "We need to get all the arrangements made."

"Why now," I ask. "Can't we wait?"

"No, it will be good to get everything done now," they say knowingly.

Off they go while I snuggle deeper into the yellow couch, listening to the lawnmowers, listening to people excitedly arriving at their summer cottages for another season. Wishing I could hear my mother's voice welcoming us for the holiday weekend.

In 24 hours, I am so grateful that my sisters took care of all the logistical details. When the end comes, you're good for nothing, but you need to get through one final hurdle that is called a funeral.

Caregiver Lesson #42

Make all the logistical arrangements before the end. When death comes, you'll be too wiped out to think logically.

44 MY MOTHER SAID THERE WOULD BE DAYS LIKE THIS

Four weeks ago, my mother told us that things would get bad as she neared the final days of her life.

As always, Bette knew what was ahead and tried to prepare her kids. Once a mother, always a mother, even when your "kids" are middle-aged adults.

"You need you to know that it will be very hard for you to care for me. Harder than anything you can imagine."

"Mum, we'll be fine, we'll be OK," I said.

"You won't be OK. But as you're going through those final days know that I will be OK. I'll be so heavily medicated that I won't be aware of the pain or any of the other awful physical things that go along with the very end."

As I lay outside Bette's bedroom all day on Friday listening to her gasping and choking on the fluid in her lungs, I remembered what she said. As I tried to put the morphine into her cheek, only to have her choke on it because she was losing the ability to swallow, I remembered what she said.

And when Bette stopped breathing altogether on Saturday afternoon, I remembered my mother told us that there would be a day like this when "the adventure would be over."

Adventures are defined as unusual or exciting experiences. There's nothing more adventurous than helping someone you love die. There's no day sadder than when they do.

Caregiver Lesson #43

There's nothing more adventurous than helping someone you love die.

45 DEW VS. FOG, SADNESS VS. GRIEF

What's the difference between dew and fog, sadness and grief?

Dew and fog are both musty, damp, cloudy. But just as they sound, they're profoundly different. As are sadness and grief.

Dew is dainty, ending in that soft "wooh" sound. Nothing serious, just a sprinkling of juicy mist. Enough to caress the lawn and moisten the leaves so they glisten when the sunlight wakes them.

Fog is a serious dude. The "ffff" sound tells you some strong and heavy vibe is coming to settle in for a while. The hard "g" sound in fog means, "Back off sister. This is my territory and I'll move on when I'm good and ready.'

Fog is like a thud, perhaps ominous, certainly preventing any plans because it's so strong and determined.

Fog, like grief, is Rambo, while the sad dew is Mary Poppins. Dew lifts by mid-morning. Fog envelops.

Caregiver Lesson #44

Get ready for Rambo-like grief to settle in and kick your ass for a while.

46 BE NICE TO THE PARROTS

When people first hear that someone is terminally ill, they send cards and leave voice mails that almost always say, "Our thoughts and prayers are with you. Let us know how we can help."

People are so kind, but "thoughts and prayers, thoughts and prayers, thoughts and prayers" starts sounding like a well-rehearsed anthem for the terminally ill. Where is people's originality, we laugh.

But the kind parrots come back at the funeral with a new anthem. The lyrics are simple: "Sorry for your loss. Sorry for your loss. Sorry for your loss."

You stand in a funeral receiving line for several hours and people come up and say "Sorry for your loss" over and over. What can you say except to parrot back, "Thank you. Appreciate you coming. Thank you. Appreciate you coming."

It's an unfulfilling exchange all around.

To the parrots – and I was one until this experience – here's a tip. Just say something simple about the person who has died. Or say how you're connected to the deceased or to the family. It makes it more interesting for the mourning family – and for you too.

Like, "I always enjoyed playing Bridge with your mother."

"We live down the street and always admired your mother's garden."

"Bette use to drive me up to my doctor in Boston."

 "I work with your brother, who's a really great guy." (Someone actually said this ,and I loved it because I learned something about my brother – and it helped me figure out how this person was connected to all of us.)

Mourning caregivers, be patient with the parrots, look them in the eye and share a kind word. Whenever possible personalize your thanks.

"Joining your Bridge Club really helped welcome my mother to the community when she moved here. Thanks for inviting her."

 "You're all mighty competitive gardeners on this street, aren't you?"

"Bette loved driving you to the doctor because she liked talking with you about books."

Lastly, remember that a funeral is only several hours long. You've done so much; you can get through this one last responsibility with dignity, graciousness, and parrots.

Caregiver Lesson #45

It's hard to talk to parrots but say something kind and personal.

47 10 TIPS FOR WRITING A KILLER EULOGY

How to write a great eulogy? Here are some tips based on my experience as a professional speechwriter, collector of great eulogies, and grieving daughter who last week wrote one for her mother.

1. **Celebrate:** try to write a eulogy that celebrates the person's life and uplifts and inspires people. When people leave a service, they want to feel good about the person they loved or cared for; they want comforting words and joyful memories that will help them bear their sadness in the days to come.

2. **Tell stories, share what you learned:** rather than simply reading a list of the person's life history and accomplishments, talk about what they meant to you and why. Or share a story that captures what the person was all about. Stories are interesting, memorable, and are much easier to talk about, especially when you're nervous. Or share three things that you learned from the person.

3. **Open with a declarative sentence or anecdote that gets attention:** paying tribute to his nephew John F. Kennedy, Jr. Sen. Ted Kennedy opened with: "Once, when they asked John what he would do if he went into politics and was elected president, he said: I guess the first thing is to call up Uncle Teddy and gloat. I loved that. It was so like his father."

4. **Be yourself:** don't worry that you don't know how to write or speak before a crowd. Just be yourself and write from your heart, not your head. Use short sentences, simple words, much like how you speak. (This will help you speak what you write, too.)   Genuine and maybe a little rough at the edges always wins out over overly-polished.

5. **Thank people**: thank people for their help, especially important if the recently deceased was ill for some period.

6. **Have a beginning, middle and end**: a good eulogy, like any good speech, starts with a point, fills in the middle with stories and anecdotes supporting that point, and concludes by reminding people of the point.

7. **Find a metaphor:** sometimes using a metaphor helps to ground the eulogy. Try to find one that is especially meaningful to the deceased. I used the metaphor of a Styrofoam swimming noodle in the eulogy for my mother. In fact, much of the first chapter of this book came from this eulogy.

8. **Keep it short**: unless you're an amazing speaker, keep the eulogy to under five minutes. As a society we're used to 15 and 30 second commercials, so even if your remarks are only a few minutes long, that's fine. It's not about length but celebrating the person's life. There's Nothing wrong with short and sweet – as long as it isn't saccharine.

9. **Practice speaking:** delivery is as important as the words. Practice reading the eulogy out loud. If some sentences seem too long, shorten them. If some words trip you up, eliminate them.

10. **Print out in large type**: Print out your speech in large type, at least 14-point font, and make it double-spaced. This will help you read it. If you can give the eulogy without reading, do it. But for most of us – especially when we feel so vulnerable and emotional – reading is a better option. And if you've practiced, it will sound good.

Caregiver Lesson #46

The best eulogies share a story or two about the deceased person and what you learned from those stories. It's like writing a letter of gratitude.

48 INSTRUCTIONS FOR THE ORPHANS

I always pictured an orphanage as a place in Ireland. Damp, dark, moldy. Cold water and scratchy blankets. Mysterious nuns and priests bossing the skinny children around all day and all night.

My life right now is the orphanage, as my caregiver duties have come to an end.

"Remember you're going to have to take care of your sisters and brothers," instructed Mum as she lay on her big white bed with the floral comforter.

"Especially watch out for Nancy. It's so hard that she's alone. It will be much easier for the rest of you because you have husbands and wives and children. I'd really like to see her move out of that neighborhood and get closer into the city where she could walk to work. Maybe you can encourage her to do that.

"Renie needs to quit her job. Maybe she can now that Tom has a new job. It's just too much for her with that big job and those little children. She can always go back to work or figure out how to do something part time.

"I'd like to see Susan teach in a different town or maybe become an art teacher. But I think she'll be OK. She's so much like Dad and Aunt Sis when she was well. So funny and interesting.

"Keep a special eye out for David and Lew. They're so sensitive and so alike. My leaving will be the hardest for them.

"Jim will be OK because he has Sarah. Petie has those beautiful grandchildren. It's so nice that she lives so close to them. Such a nice family. And Betty takes good care of Bill.

"You will help them, won't you?"

"Yes, Mum, I will."

"And I want you to call everyone every week."

"Yes, Mum, you know I will. I'll call everyone and make sure we're all together on Thanksgiving and Christmas, too"

"Good, that makes me feel so much better. But wait, who will take care of you?"

Good question, I thought. You're not supposed to be dying so young, Mum. And why is it that I always have to be so damn responsible. But I snapped out of my internal whining and said, "You know Greg and Ian take good care of me."

"Yes, especially that Ian," said Mum. "You know I met him in a dream before he was born. He came up to me and said, 'I know you. You're my Nanie.' I wish I could have lived to see all these grandchildren grow up. I always thought I'd be at their weddings or at least their high school graduations."

Before she died bossy Bette made sure that everyone would be taken care of when she no longer could.

My sister Nancy called last night.

"Mum told me to make sure I would call at least once a week," said Nancy. "You know I'm not much of a talker during the week because I'm so tired from work. But let's talk on the weekends."

After we hung up, I smiled. Bette had spread the instructions around.

I called Petie, Bette's sister, the next night to see how she was.

"I'm having a hard time, Lo. A really hard time. Your mother was always so concerned about the boys. I think they're alright, but I'm not."

"The hardest part," said Petie, "Is that I miss her bossing me around."

If we follow the final instructions, like obeying the nuns' and priests' orders in that imaginary Irish orphanage, we'll still get the glow of lovingly being bossed around by the person we no longer have.

Caregiver Lesson #47

Obey the final instructions.

49 ASHES TO ASHES, DUST TO JOY

There we were on the beach saying a prayer, just Bette's children and sister and brothers with the wonderful Rev. Paige Fisher on a cloudy, 60-degree Saturday morning.

Then there we were in the icy cold Cape Cod water, flinging Bette's ashes every which way, yelping like sea lion pups. Laughing. Screaming from the cold. Smiling from a joy that blew in from who knows where.

We thought this day would be unbearably sad, our final goodbye. Instead the day was a release.

We put Mum's ashes into small plastic cups, swam out and flung them into the unusually gentle June winds, along with our grief. No need for swimming noodles today.

This is exactly what Bette would have wanted. All of us together, finding happiness instead of moping around. Sometimes it bothered us that Bette would block difficult memories, talking only about the good, dismissing those who insisted on dwelling on the negative as "ridiculous."

Now we know.

Grieving is so personal. There's no advice I can share, really, except to reflect on how the person you have lost lived life at his or her best and make those qualities part of your life. It's the greatest praise to the deceased, and the greatest gift to yourself.

Caregiver Lesson #48

Take the best parts of the person you loved and make them your own. Toss everything else to the wind.

50 WRITING DOWN YOUR GRIEF

Psychology studies have found that writing about stressful, traumatic or emotional events, like caring for a dying person or grieving their loss, helps people more quickly recover, both psychologically and physically.

Professor James Pennebaker, a psychology professor at the University of Texas, provides these suggestions for writing down your grief:

1. Find a time and place where you won't be disturbed. Ideally, pick a time at the end of your workday or before you go to bed.

2. Promise yourself that you will write for a minimum of 15 minutes a day for at least 3 or 4 consecutive days.

3. Once you begin writing, write continuously. Don't worry about spelling or grammar. If you run out of things to write about, just repeat what you have already written.

4. You can write long-hand, or you can type on a computer. If you are unable to write, you can also record yourself.

5. You can write about the same thing on all 3-4 days of writing or you can write about something different each day. It is entirely up to you.

6. Whatever you chose to write about, however, it is critical that you really let go and explore your very deepest emotions and thoughts.

Poet David Whyte on losing his mother

In *Farewell Letter*, a poem that Poet David Whyte wrote after his mother's death, he writes of receiving an imaginary letter from his mother after her death. The end of the poem reads:

I know your generous soul is well able to let me go

you will in the end be happy to know my God was true and I find myself

after loving you all so long, in the wide,

infinite mercy

of being mothered myself.

PS -- All your intuitions were true.

My uncle Lew Newell wrote this about losing his sister Bette:

It's a gorgeous day. The sun is bright and warming. A great day for my walk at South Cape Beach. My thoughts turn to Bet as I knew the beach would do.

As I continued my walk looking for sea glass it became frustrating. Nothing.

I know what, I'll just ask Bet and she will turn up a beautiful piece of glass.

But still nothing. (Where are you Bet?)

I know you are here, give me a sign. Still nothing. (Where are you Bet?)

I couldn't understand why there was no reply, no signal, no sign.

As I started to return, I noticed two colorful sea ducks along the water's edge.

Gulls overhead floated in the breeze with grace.

The terns and plovers overhead squawked and warned me away from their nests.

The sun glimmered off the ocean, the Vineyard nearby.

Bet was everywhere around me and I finally noticed. I no longer need to ask (Where are you Bet?)

And me? Well, by writing down the stories in this book every night while caring for my mother, I stayed sane and learned one or ten things about myself, my mother and my family. Rereading these stories has helped me grieve and heal.

Caregiver Lesson #49

Writing how you feel will help you heal.

51 THOSE COMPETITIVE KENNEDYS

I had such a flashback when news broke that Ted Kennedy had died of brain cancer eight weeks after Bette died.

I remembered the day in the 1970s when Ted Kennedy came to the suburban Boston newspaper where I worked after school taking classified ads over the phone and writing obituaries and wedding announcements. I remember how gracious, funny and generous he was, making time to talk to me, a skinny little 14-year-old kid with big ambitions and coke-bottle glasses.

My mother, a federal housing administrator, would tell us about her meetings with Ted Kennedy. She would often be infuriated after them because Kennedy was so liberal, but she always said she respected our Massachusetts senator.

"The remarkable thing," said Bette, "is that Ted Kennedy truly cares about how these issues affect people. Sure, he's a politician, but a politician in the best ways."

The real reason she admired Ted Kennedy, though, was because he was always asking to use her office to make a couple of phone calls. (This being pre-mobile phone days.)

Bette could hear his booming voice talking to one of his children or nieces or nephews. His voice changed from the politician to the father, from the orator to Uncle Ted. His humanness and kindness were the qualities Bette respected and that she herself had in abundance.

Bette lived on Cape Cod near Kennedy and shared his wish to be cared for by family at their beach houses as brain cancer marched them to the close.

Bette would often ask me, "Is Ted Kennedy still alive this week? Good, maybe I can live a few more months with this disease too."

Ted made it longer than my mother, but those Kennedy's are such over-achievers.

I hope I can remember to be as generous and caring as my mother and Ted Kennedy. We all screw up in life, but a passion for helping others is a life well lived.

Caregiver Lesson #50

When you help someone die, you develop a greater capacity to love, be loved, and experience joy. (You can do it, really.)

ABOUT THE AUTHOR

Lois Kelly is the author of several books, including "Rebels at Work: A Handbook for Leading Change Within." She works with Fortune 500 clients to develop the capacity to innovate and adapt to change. Lois lives in Rhode Island with her husband. Lois was the oldest of Bette Kelly's six children.

Elizabeth (Bette) Kelly, the inspiration for *Be the Noodle,* lived at Popponesset Beach in Mashpee, Mass. She was the mother of six, wife, sister, aunt and friend. She asked her daughter Lois to write about her end- of-life "adventure" in hope of helping others who are in the same boat.

Printed in Great Britain
by Amazon

41020978R00067